by

Dennis P. Eichhorn

A *Reading Success* Paperback Book

Turman Publishing Company
Seattle

Author: Dennis P. Eichhorn

Series Editor: Louise Morgan

Copy Editor: Lori Starrs

Photo Credits: AP/Wide World Photos, Paramount Pictures,
Pictorial Parade, Retna, Twentieth Century-Fox

Harris-Jacobson Rating 4

An Unauthorized Biography

Copyright © 1987 Turman Publishing Company
1319 Dexter Avenue North
Seattle, Washington 98109
All rights reserved.

Catalog No. 207
Library of Congress Catalog Card Number: 88-50794
ISBN 0-89872-207-1
Printed in the United States of America.

CONTENTS

NOTE: A glossary of unfamiliar terms is provided at the end of each chapter.

Tom Cruise may be the most popular young movie star in the world.

CHAPTER **1**

"I really do love my work."

"**I**'m lucky," says Tom Cruise. "Very lucky. I'm doing something that I love to do." In just a few short years, Tom has become one of the world's best-known actors. He's a movie star now, and he gets paid more than $1 million for every film he makes. Yes, a lot of people would agree that Tom is a lucky man, but there is more to Tom's success than luck. He has worked very hard to become a good actor.

"I don't know my limits as an actor yet," Tom admits. "This is just the beginning. I'm exploring. People should realize that I'm still growing as an actor. I try to learn from my mistakes. I am thankful for what I have. I don't think about the past. I think about tomorrow.

"I really do love my work. I love acting. I'm working toward a long-range goal of my potential as an artist. I know what I want to be. I don't want to be the next James Dean. That's already been done. Do I want to be a big star? Well, if being a star means that you're someone people will go to see in films . . . yes, I want that.

"I'm a serious person. As I said, I feel that I've been very lucky, but acting is only one part of my life. Even though I love my work, my family is very important to me, too. What could be more important than your family?"

Tom's one of the new breed of young actors who have shot to the top in a short time. Tom didn't spend years as a stage actor. He didn't study acting in college. Instead, he broke into films quickly. After Tom's first part in the film *Endless Love,* most people didn't know who he was. But after *Taps,* his second film, people began to realize that Tom was a fine actor. Then came *Risky Business.* Suddenly Tom was a star.

Some of Tom's films haven't made money. *Losin' It* and *Legend* were not big hits. But Tom learned a lot from making those movies. His other films have done very well. *All The Right Moves, Top Gun,* and *The Color Of Money* have made Tom a major star. People have seen from these films that Tom is a hard-working and talented actor.

Tom knows that, for an actor, he's in a good spot. "The biggest benefit from being lucky enough to be in hit movies is that now I can pick and choose what I want to do," he says. "That's what it means. I want to learn my craft and I want to be in good movies. In order to have that freedom, you have to have at least one money-making hit. After that happened for me, things got better.

"I want to keep my characters fresh. To do that, I have to keep trying new things. I've learned how to turn parts down. I'm successful, and I don't question my success. If what I'm doing is working, I don't question it."

People know Tom for the parts he has played in movies. They remember him as the tough military cadet in *Taps.* He was the high school senior in *Risky Business,* the star football player in *All The Right Moves,* the troubled teenager in *The Outsiders,* the awesome fighter pilot in *Top Gun,* and the great pool player in *The Color Of Money.* To Tom's many fans, he will always be the characters that he has played in his movies. Most people will never know what Tom is like as a person.

The real Tom Cruise is a very interesting young man. He hasn't wasted much time. Once Tom discovered what he wanted to do with his life, he gave it his best shot. This is the story of how it happened.

In **All The Right Moves,** *Tom plays Stef, a senior high school football player hoping to land an athletic scholarship.*

"I really do love my work."

Glossary

This glossary gives an explanation of how certain words were used in this book. A more complete definition of each word can be found in a dictionary.

actors: people who play parts in movies and plays.

admits: says.

artist: a creative person.

awesome: wonderful, great.

benefit: good result.

best shot: best effort.

breed: group.

broke: entered suddenly.

characters: people in stories.

craft: skill.

discovered: found out.

exploring: trying new things.

freedom: ability to do what he wants.

fresh: new.

important: means a lot.

limits: what is possible.

long-range: far in the future.

major: big.

military cadet: someone training to be in the armed forces.

mistakes: what he has done wrong.

money-making: something that makes money.

pilot: a person who flies planes.

potential: what he can do.
question: try to figure out.
realize: know, understand.
serious: thinks about what is important.
short: quick.
shot: gone quickly.
spot: place.
stage: place where plays are done.
success: doing well.
talented: has natural ability.
thankful: happy.
tough: strong, does not give in.
wasted: thrown away.

CHAPTER 2

"I was always the new kid."

Thomas Cruise Mapother IV was born in Syracuse, New York, on July 3, 1962. His mother, Mary Lee, had once been an actress. His father, Thomas Cruise Mapother III, was an inventor and electrical engineer. There were four children in the Mapother family, and Tom was the third. He has three sisters: Marian, Lee Anne, and Cass.

The family moved quite often because of the work Tom's father did. From Syracuse, they moved to New Jersey, then to Ottawa, Canada, then to St. Louis, Missouri. Then it was back to New Jersey with side trips to Kentucky and Ohio. "I went to eight different grade schools and three high schools," Tom remembers. "I was always the new kid, always trying to fight my way in to get some love and attention.

"I never lived in one place for very long. I was always packing and moving someplace else. I was very frustrated while I was growing up. I didn't have a lot of friends. The people closest to me were my family. I guess you could say that I felt kind of scattered."

7

School was hard for Tom because he had a hard time reading. He was born with dyslexia, a reading disability. His mother and sisters all had the same problem. "I first became aware of it in kindergarten," says Tom. "I didn't know if letters like 'C' or 'D' curved to the left or to the right. That affects everything you do in school. My spelling was terrible. Reading was extremely difficult because it took me so long.

"I was put into remedial reading classes everywhere I went. When you're a new kid, as I always seemed to be, all you want to do is blend in with everything and make friends. I couldn't do that. I felt singled out. It was a real drag."

Tom's mother worked long hours with him to help him overcome dyslexia. "It's 100 percent better now," he says. "I've learned how to control my eyes. I used to have to use my finger to read; otherwise I'd skip lines and words. I just wasn't relaxed about it. It no longer affects me, but it did have a big influence on my life while I was growing up."

Even as a little boy, Tom loved to act. "He used to make up skits," his mother remembers. "He'd pretend to be Donald Duck, Woody Woodpecker, and W. C. Fields when he was just a tiny tot. I guess I was his greatest audience. The desire to act was in him, even then. But as Tom got older, he was into sports more, and the acting stopped for a while."

"I was always the new kid."

Tom was one of several recipients of the Outstanding Learning Disabled Achiever Award presented by Mrs. Reagan at the White House. Tom is shown here with Olympic gold-medalist Bruce Jenner and actress/singer Cher.

"I wanted to fit in, and sports seemed like a good way to do that," says Tom. "Wherever we moved, I picked up a different sport. It was a good way to make friends. I threw myself headfirst into every sport I tried: wrestling, hockey, lacrosse, tennis, football, baseball, and skiing. I'd go up to people and say something like, 'Do you play tennis? Do you want to play sometime?'"

When Tom was 11 years old, his parents were divorced. He and his sisters moved to Kentucky with their mother. It was a hard time for Tom. "After the divorce, I felt very vulnerable," he says. "I closed myself off a lot from people. I didn't think the other kids understood me. They hadn't had the same kind of childhood that I had. I needed and wanted love and attention from people. I felt like I wasn't fitting in at all."

Tom spent his high school freshman year at a Catholic boarding school. "I needed to focus my life," he says. "The people at St. Francis Seminary in Cincinnati accepted me, so I spent a session there studying with the Franciscans. I left when it just didn't seem to fit my needs anymore."

When Tom was 16, his mother remarried. "At first, I felt threatened by my stepfather," he says. "But he was such a wise, smart man that I got over it. He loved my mother so much that he took in all four of us kids." The family moved to Glen Ridge, New Jersey.

Tom kept busy with athletics. He turned out for wrestling during his senior year and injured his knee. Tom didn't know it at the time, but that knee injury was a turning point in his life.

"I had been a singer in the glee club," Tom says. "So when I couldn't wrestle anymore, a teacher suggested that I try out for the school play, *Guys And Dolls.* I went out for it, and I got the part of Nathan Detroit. I found out that I loved acting."

Tom felt misunderstood and vulnerable as a young man. He kept busy with athletics until a knee injury led him to a beginning in drama. "I found out that I loved acting," says Tom.

"I was always the new kid."

Glossary

This glossary gives an explanation of how certain words were used in this book. A more complete definition of each word can be found in a dictionary.

accepted me: let attend.

actress: woman who acts.

athletics: sports.

attention: notice from other people.

audience: people who watch and listen.

baseball: sport played between two teams with a bat and ball.

blend in: fit in.

boarding school: school with live-in students.

childhood: the time he was a child.

closest people: people who knew him best.

control: having power over.

curved: bending one way.

divorced: split up; separated.

drag: bad time.

dyslexia: problem that makes reading difficult.

electrical engineer: person with a technical job.

extremely: very.

focus: direct his energy toward something.

football: body contact game played between two teams.

Franciscans: certain religious group.

freshman: first year.

frustrated: unhappy.

headfirst: with everything he had.

hockey: sport played on ice.

influence: something that affected him.

injured: hurt.

inventor: person who creates new things.

kid: child.

kindergarten: school for four- and five-year-olds.

lacrosse: an old Indian sport.

often: many times.

overcome: get over.

packing: putting things in boxes.

pretend: act out a part.

relaxed: rested.

remedial: needing extra help.

scattered: tossed about.

seminary: religious training school.

session: school year.

side trips: other places visited.

singled out: apart from others; alone.

skip: miss; not see.

skits: very short plays.

someplace: other places.

sports: games.

stepfather: man, other than natural father, who married his mother.

suggested: gave someone the idea.

tennis: sport where players hit a ball across a net.

threatened: feeling that he might be hurt.

tiny tot: little child.

turning point: point after which everything changes.

vulnerable: easily hurt.

wrestling: body contact sport played between two people.

CHAPTER **3**

"It felt right."

Tom had discovered acting. "I remember feeling so at home onstage in *Guys And Dolls*," he says. "I was so relaxed. I really enjoyed it. It felt right, and I said to myself, 'This is where I'm at.' After some of the guys I knew saw the play, they came around and said, 'Hey, we didn't know you could do that.' I felt good about it. Not about the fact that they'd seen it . . . I just felt good about it in my heart."

Tom's family watched the play, too. They loved what they saw. "I can't describe the feelings I had," says Tom's mother. "It was just an incredible experience. We could see a lot of talent coming forth all of a sudden. It had been hidden for so many years. We hadn't thought about it or talked about it in any way before that night. Then to see Tom onstage . . . it was wonderful."

After the show, Tom came home and talked to his parents. He had been planning to travel through Europe after high school, but now he had changed his mind. "I want to give acting a try," Tom told his parents. "I'm going to give it 10 years.

Let me see if I can make it as an actor. I really feel that this is what I want to do."

"We both agreed with him," Tom's mother says. "We felt that he had a God-given talent. We felt he should explore it because he was so excited about it. We gave him our blessing, and the rest is history."

Tom got a part in the play *Godspell* at a local dinner theater. "I knew I had made the right decision," he says. "Acting was a better way for me to express myself than sports. I felt so great onstage that I couldn't get enough of it. I decided to move to New York City and get serious about acting."

Living in New York takes money. The money Tom had saved for Europe got him started although it didn't last very long. Soon he was like the thousands of other young actors in the big city. Tom worked at many different jobs to support himself. He waited tables, unloaded trucks, and sold ice cream. When he wasn't working, Tom went to plays, participated in acting workshops, and tried out for parts in plays and movies. He also found himself an agent who helped him look for work.

Five months after moving to New York, Tom got his first part in a movie. It was a small part in *Endless Love,* which starred Brooke Shields and Martin Newitt. Even though it was only one day's work, it was a beginning.

"It felt right."

A great old pro, Dustin Hoffman shares a joke with the hottest new actor in the business.

Glossary

This glossary gives an explanation of how certain words were used in this book. A more complete definition of each word can be found in a dictionary.

agent: person who helped him find work.

blessing: approval; permission.

coming forth: showing up.

decided: chose to do.

decision: what he chose to do.

describe: tell; explain.

experience: something that happened.

express: tell.

God-given talent: ability someone is born with.

heart: true self.

hidden: not seen.

history: past events.

incredible: wonderful; amazing.

participated: took part in.

relaxed: not afraid.

serious: dedicated; intense.

support: make money to live on.

travel: visit new places.

waited tables: worked at a restaurant taking orders.

workshops: short classes.

CHAPTER **4**

"I believed in myself."

"I don't think I even met Brooke Shields," Tom says. "I went to the audition just as a lark. I went to every audition I could for parts that were for actors my age, and this was one of them. There weren't that many. It was just a little walk on, but it taught me where the camera was, and it got me in a movie. Once you're in one, you can go to other auditions and at least say that you've done something other than amateur theater."

Tom continued trying to find work as an actor. He was turned down many times. Tom didn't let that get him down. "I felt that the people who were turning me down were there to help me in the long run," he says. "Sometimes it hurt, but I truly believed that there were parts I was supposed to get and parts I wasn't meant to have. I knew that something else would come along.

"I remember being flown out to Los Angeles to read for a part in a TV series. I didn't know anything about acting in L.A.; I didn't know how tough it was. I went in to read for a director who thought he was the coolest thing happening. After

I read for the part, I knew I was terrible. He said, 'So, how long are you going to be in California?' I thought to myself, 'He's probably going to want me to come back and read again with someone else.' I said, 'Well, just a couple of days.' And he said 'Good. Get a tan while you're here.' I walked out, and I thought it was the funniest thing that had ever happened to me. I was laughing so hard that tears were coming out of my eyes. I thought, 'This is Hollywood. Welcome, Cruise.' "

Tom soon learned how some of the things that had been problems for him in school were helping him as an actor. "Because I was dyslexic, I had developed a very good memory," he says. "And because we had moved around a lot, I had picked up quite a few accents. I had had such extremes in my life: I had been kind of a wild kid, and then I had spent a year studying to become a Franciscan priest. All of this personal experience helped me as an actor.

"Also, I was very aggressive. I knew what I wanted to do. I believed in myself even when it was tough getting started. If I hadn't had such a rough childhood, I might have given up. But I was used to overcoming hard times."

A few months after working in *Endless Love*, Tom got his second part in a movie. This time, he had a larger part. The name of the movie was *Taps*.

"I believed in myself."

Like many young actors, Tom had a hard time finding work, but he says, "I believed in myself even when it was tough getting started. I was used to overcoming hard times."

Glossary

This glossary gives an explanation of how certain words were used in this book. A more complete definition of each word can be found in a dictionary.

accents: different ways of speaking.

aggressive: with a lot of energy and force.

amateur: not very good at something.

audition: a try out.

continued: kept on.

coolest: greatest; most important.

couple: a few.

developed: formed.

director: person in charge of a movie.

extremes: opposites.

happening: going on.

lark: something done for the fun of it.

memory: what he can remember.

overcoming: getting over something.

priest: a leader in a church.

rough: difficult; hard.

tan: brown skin color caused by the sun.

terrible: really bad.

tough: hard to do.

walk on: small part in a play or movie.

CHAPTER **5**

"I thought anyone could make a great movie."

Taps was a big step forward for Tom. It was a movie about life in a military school. Timothy Hutton and Sean Penn were to be the stars. At first, Tom was chosen to play the part of a friend of David Shawn, a cadet at the school. But the actor who was supposed to play David Shawn wasn't working out. "Tom was so strong that the other guy didn't have a chance," says Sean Penn. "Tom was very intense and very overpowering." After a few days, director Harold Becker offered the part of David Shawn to Tom.

Tom knew this was a big break. "I felt like it was a chance for me to show what I could do," he says. "It was a special time in my life, because it was my first real part in a movie. It was Sean's first movie, too. Timothy Hutton had just won an Academy award, and he was all excited. We all felt something special was happening.

"For me to bring any character to life, he has to be part of me. I put a lot of the fear that I felt

Tom knew that his part in Taps was a big break for him; "It was a special time in my life, because it was my first real part in a movie."

in my childhood into the way I played David Shawn. He was afraid, so he got into fights.

"David Shawn wasn't in many scenes, so I wanted him to make a real impact. It was my idea to get a crew cut and gain 15 pounds for the part. I was much heavier for that role than for any other role I've done. I drank a lot of milkshakes and worked out until I bulked up to the size that I thought my character needed to be."

Tom got a lot of attention for his work in *Taps*. He was soon offered another part in a movie. Tom took it but later wished he hadn't. "At first, the movie was called *Tijuana*," explains Tom. "I didn't want to do it, but everyone said that I needed more exposure. Besides, I wasn't offered anything else." The film, which was finally named *Losin' It*, was a dumb comedy about some high school kids who go to a Mexican border town to have a good time. *Losin' It* was a flop and wasn't seen by many people.

"Making *Losin' It* was the most depressing experience of my life up to that point," says Tom. "I'll never make another film like that. But it was an eye-opener for me. I began to understand that you really have to be careful about what you do. You may feel that you can make a script into something good, but you've got to take a close look at everything that goes into a movie. Who's producing? Who's directing?

"Looking back on *Losin' It*, I can see that it was an important film for me. Now, I can look at it

and say, 'Thank God I've grown.' I thought anyone could make a great movie and that all you had
to do was just knock yourself out. I worked hard
on it, but there was no hope. I learned a lot from
that experience. After *Losin' It*, I turned down
several similar scripts. People told me I'd better
take a chance and turn some things down. If I
didn't, that would be all that I was offered. They
turned out to be right."

So Tom found himself a new agent. "I told
myself, 'I have to work with good people and good
directors so that I can grow' " he says. "Because
of my work in *Taps,* I was getting a lot of offers
to play killers in horror films. I didn't want to go
in that direction. I remember telling my agent that
I wanted to work with Francis Ford Coppola. He
said, 'Francis! He's not going to pay you anything!'
But I still wanted to be in one of his films."

Francis Ford Coppola had directed many great
films such as *The Godfather* and *Apocalypse Now.*
Tom learned that Francis was getting ready to
make a film called *The Outsiders.* "When I heard
about it, I went to Los Angeles to talk with
Francis," says Tom. "I told him, 'Look, I don't care
what role you give me. I really want to work with
you. I want to be there on the set and watch,' and
he said 'okay.' "

Tom had gone from *Losin' It* to *The Outsiders.*
It was definitely a step in the right direction.

"I thought anyone could make a great movie."

Tom didn't care what role he got in The Outsiders; *he just told director Francis Ford Coppola, "I really want to work with you." Tom is shown here with co-stars C. Thomas Howell (left) and Emilio Estevez (right).*

Glossary

This glossary gives an explanation of how certain words were used in this book. A more complete definition of each word can be found in a dictionary.

break: lucky chance.

bulked up: built up muscles.

cadet: student at a military school.

chance: ability to do something.

character: person in a story.

crew cut: very short haircut.

definitely: for sure.

depressing experience: sad time.

exposure: being seen by a lot of people.

eye-opener: experience that made him realize something.

fear: feeling that something bad will happen.

flop: complete failure.

grown: gained experience.

heavier: had put on weight.

horror films: scary movies.

impact: something people will be sure to remember.

intense: very moving; deep.

knock yourself out: work hard.

learned: found out.

military school: strict school where students train as if they were in the armed forces.

offered: asked him if he wanted it.

"I thought anyone could make a great movie."

overpowering: strong; powerful.

role: part an actor plays.

scenes: different places in a movie or play.

script: what actors say, written down.

several: many.

special: exciting.

step forward: event that took him closer to his goal.

supposed: was going to.

CHAPTER **6**

"I knew this could be good."

*T*he *Outsiders* was based on a book by S. E. Hinton about teenage gangs in Oklahoma. It was one of Tom's favorite books, and Francis Ford Coppola was one of his favorite directors. When Francis gave Tom the part of a service station attendant in the film, it was like a dream come true for the young actor. "There I was, 19 years old and working with one of the greatest directors in the world," Tom says. "I was acting with people like Matt Dillon, Rob Lowe, and Emilio Estevez. I had a great time.

"My part wasn't much, but I created something with it. I learned that I had a sense of comedy. Francis let us ad-lib and make things up as we went along. He was like one of the guys. There we were, a group of actors in the middle of Oklahoma making a movie. I'll never forget it."

While Tom was working on *The Outsiders,* he flew to Los Angeles to take care of some business. Director Paul Brickman was getting ready to film *Risky Business* and invited Tom to try out for the

"If we ain't got each other, we ain't got nuthin'," was the motto for this gang from **The Outsiders**. *Members included Emilio Estevez, Rob Lowe, C. Thomas Howell, Matt Dillon, Ralph Macchio, Patrick Swayze, and Tom.*

lead role, Joel Goodsen. "I went in to meet Paul just to say hello," says Tom. "He had seen me in *Taps* but didn't know if I'd be right for *Risky Business*. I was into the character I was playing in *The Outsiders*: I went in wearing a jean jacket, my tooth was chipped, and my hair was greasy. I was all pumped up from lifting weights, and I had a tattoo. This was all for my character in *The Outsiders*. I didn't look a thing like Joel was supposed to be like in *Risky Business*.

"I said, 'Hey, how y'all doing?' in my Oklahoma accent. Paul Brickman just sat there looking at me. Then he said, 'Let's just read a little bit.' Now I'm not a very good cold reader. Usually, I start with a line and go off and ad-lib, finding my way down the script. But this time I started reading the script.

"I went a little ways, and then I stopped and said, 'Let me try it again another way.' I didn't know it at the time, but they were ready to say, 'Okay, good-bye and thank-you very much.' But I started from the top again and did it another way. We ended up reading through half the script. It was great fun. We were all laughing."

Paul Brickman was interested in Tom for the part, but he wasn't sure. Tom went back to Oklahoma to finish *The Outsiders*. "I didn't really think that *Risky Business* would be anything special until I read the whole script," Tom says. "It just floated. I knew this could be good. But still, in the back of my mind, I was afraid that it could be another *Losin' It*."

Tom agreed to be tested for *Risky Business* again. Finally, Paul Brickman offered him the part of Joel. Suddenly, Tom was faced with a tough choice. "The same week that Paul offered me the part of Joel, Francis offered everyone in *The Outsiders* a part in his next movie, *Rumble Fish*. I decided to go with *Risky Business* because I would play the lead. In *Rumble Fish* I would have been just one of the guys. If I'd never been in a Coppola film, I would have said yes to Francis. But I thought Paul Brickman was a very bright guy with great taste. He knew exactly what the movie was going to be, and I went with him. I think Francis was a little surprised. If I got the chance, I'd work for Francis again in a minute."

Tom began working on the part of Joel Goodsen. *Risky Business* is about a young man who is graduating from high school and getting ready to go to college. His parents leave him home alone while they go on a trip. Joel manages to get in every possible kind of trouble. But he pulls things together before his folks return, and everything turns out all right in the end.

To prepare for the part of Joel, Tom lost 14 pounds by jogging and going on a diet. After he reached the weight he wanted, Tom stopped exercising. "I wanted to put on a little layer of baby fat," he explains. "Joel is a very vulnerable person. I didn't want him to look like he had any physical defenses.

"I knew this could be good."

Tom *and Rebecca DeMornay, his co-star from* **Risky Business**, *celebrate the finishing of the film.*

"Joel is the kind of person who worries about the future. He's under a lot of pressure, yet he's still asking questions. What about America? What about the human race? Do you want to help people, or is life just about making money? Those are the same things that kids coming out of high school now are asking. For Joel, those questions take him through the movie to explore his feelings. He gets sucked into this wild ride, but he never sells out."

When *Risky Business* came out, it was a big hit. Tom was a star at last. People began to recognize him on the street. At first, Tom had a hard time getting used to being famous. "I'm really a very private person," he says. "All at once people were staring at me wherever I went."

"I knew this could be good."

Glossary

This glossary gives an explanation of how certain words were used in this book. A more complete definition of each word can be found in a dictionary.

ad-lib: make up as he goes along.
attendant: worker at the gas station.
based on: used to make the movie.
chipped: broken.
cold reader: reading for the first time.
created: made something new.
diet: eating less.
exactly: has thought about every little thing.
exercising: doing physical fitness activities.
explains: tells about.
explore: look at up close.
famous: well known.
favorite: thing he likes best.
forget: not remember.
future: what's going to happen.
gangs: groups of tough kids.
graduating: finishing school.
greasy: slicked down.
interested: thought he might be good.
invited: asked to do.
jogging: running for exercise.
lifting weights: exercise that makes muscles
  stronger.
physical defenses: ability to fight back.

pressure: a feeling that he's being forced into something.

private: enjoys being alone.

pumped up: with built-up muscles.

recognize: knew who he was.

return: come back.

sells out: quits doing what's right.

sense of comedy: a feel for funny things.

staring: looking and not saying anything.

sucked: pulled into.

suddenly: all at once.

taste: knowing the right way to do things.

tested: try out.

tough choice: a decision that's hard to make.

vulnerable: easily hurt.

worries: is afraid about what will happen.

CHAPTER **7**

"I'll let my work speak for itself."

Tom was hot. In the 1980s, a lot of young actors were making names for themselves, and Tom was one of them. Many of these young stars—Tom, Sean Penn, Rob Lowe, Emilio Estevez, Judd Nelson, and Matt Dillon—were friends. Whenever any of these young stars got together, they soon became the center of attention. Before long, people began calling them "The Brat Pack."

Tom didn't like that very much. "It's just something that the press made up," he says. "I want no part of it. Putting me in there is stupid. We all have different personalities. I don't like it because I work hard to be an actor with my own style, and then someone comes along and lumps me in with a bunch of other people. Now I've gotten used to the name. When people talk like that, it doesn't bother me anymore. I know where I am. I do my work, and I'll let it speak for itself."

There was a lot of work for Tom. As soon as *Risky Business* was finished, he went right to work on another movie. It was called *All The Right Moves.* Once again, Tom was the star. He played

Tom was just clowning around with Rob Lowe (left) and Emilio Estevez (right) at the screening of Emilio's TV movie **In The Custody Of Strangers.**

the part of Stef Djordjevic, a high school senior who is a football star. Stef hopes to win a football scholarship so he can go to college and study engineering. Then Stef gets into an argument with his coach and is kicked off the team before the last game of the year. Even though it doesn't look as if he'll get a scholarship, everything turns out all right in the end.

Tom worked hard to turn himself into Stef. He went into football training. Tom also went on a meat-and-potatoes diet, gaining back most of the weight he had lost playing the part of Joel. He dyed his hair black. Soon, Tom began to look the part.

All The Right Moves was being filmed in Johnstown, Pennsylvania, so Tom spent several weeks living there. He wanted to get an idea of what it would be like to grow up in a steel town. Tom met kids like Stef. "Stef is hungry," says Tom. "Joel came from a very secure, upper-middle-class background. He always had money, so he could take the time to question things and discover what life was all about. But Stef comes from a depressed steel town in Pennsylvania. It's a place where the youth don't have many opportunities.

"Stef has the point of view that college is the only way he can get what he wants. So he has set definite goals for himself. He uses his ability on the football field as a way out. He doesn't have the money to go to college, so he has to earn a football scholarship. Otherwise, he'll wind up staying in his hometown trying to get a job at the steel mill."

Tom played in all of the football scenes in the movie. His experience as an athlete came in handy. "I went to practice with the kids from the town for two-and-a-half weeks," Tom says. "It was fun, but it was hard work."

The weather was bad, and partway through the making of the movie Tom caught a cold. He had to keep working even though he had a fever. "I ended up losing all of the weight I had gained for the part," Tom says. "For a couple of weeks after I was better, I had to wear extra clothing so that I'd still look beefed up."

In spite of his being sick, Tom did a great job of acting. *All The Right Moves* was another big hit for him. Tom began getting more offers than ever to act in films. Tom took his time deciding what to do next. He had learned the hard way to be careful. Tom was interested in a movie that director Ridley Scott was preparing to make in England. Finally, he decided to take the lead role in it. The movie was to be called *Legend*.

"I liked the part that was offered to me," Tom says. "I had already played all the extremes of high school life. In *Legend*, I would be this magical character, Jack O' The Green. Besides, I was having a hard time getting used to everyone looking at me wherever I went. It seemed like the perfect time to get out of the country and go to England."

Then something happened that gave him a lot more to think about. There was a death in his family. Tom was in Los Angeles getting ready to leave for England when he got the news that his father had died.

"I'll let my work speak for itself."

In **All The Right Moves,** *both Tom and his co-star Lea Thompson, promised mutual support toward realizing their dreams for college.*

Glossary

This glossary gives an explanation of how certain words were used in this book. A more complete definition of each word can be found in a dictionary.

argument: fight.

beefed up: with built-up muscles.

bother: make him mad.

Brat Pack: group of famous young actors.

center of attention: what everyone notices.

definite: fixed.

depressed: poor.

diet: what he ate.

discover: find out.

dyed: made a different color.

extremes: opposites.

fever: sickness.

filmed: made.

gaining: putting on.

handy: useful.

hot: very popular.

in spite of: even though.

kicked off: taken off; not allowed to play.

lumps: includes without thinking.

magical: make-believe; like magic.

meat-and-potatoes: basic; not fancy.

opportunities: what is possible to do.

otherwise: if things work out in a different way.

perfect: great; exactly right.

"I'll let my work speak for itself."

personalities: how people act.

point of view: belief.

practice: play to get better.

press: people working for newspapers, radio, and TV.

scholarship: money given to him to attend school.

secure: safe.

speak for itself: show on its own how good it is.

steel town: town where many people work in steel mills.

study engineering: learn to be an engineer.

stupid: dumb.

style: own way of doing something.

upper-middle-class: from a group of people who make more money than most.

youth: young people.

CHAPTER 8

"I don't want to make another movie like that again."

Tom's father had been ill for quite a while. He'd had a cancer operation just after *All The Right Moves* came out, and Tom and his three sisters had gone to visit their father in the hospital. It had been several years since they'd seen their father, but they wanted to do all they could to show their concern. It was a hard time for everyone in Tom's family.

"When my father died," Tom says, "I think that he felt bad about a lot of what had happened. He was a person who did not have a huge influence on me in my teens. My goals and reasons for wanting to succeed really came from my stepfather. But my father was important to me. Really important. It's hard to explain."

Tom was glad that he'd decided to be in *Legend*. "After what I was going through emotionally, facing my father's death, it was important for me to get back to the innocence within my own soul," he says. "I'm just glad I had acting to fall back

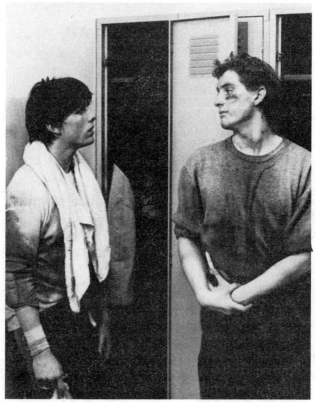

As high school seniors, Tom and co-star Christopher Penn were both seeking an athletic scholarship. It was their only way out of a depressed steel town in Pennsylvania.

on. I don't know what I would have done without my work. By working I had a way to deal with all those emotions."

Ridley Scott, the director of *Legend*, also had directed *Alien* and *Blade Runner*. Tom was anxious to work with him. "Ridley wanted to make a fairy tale," says Tom. "He had a dream, and my character was really just a bit of color in his dream. I looked at the script for *Legend* and knew that it was the scariest project anyone had offered me. I felt that it would be very hard physically. It was going to be a real challenge."

Tom's character was a forest man who loves a princess, plays with fairies and elves, and battles a creature named Darkness. "I knew what I was getting into," Tom says. "It was a challenge both because of the character and because it was a special-effects film. Sometimes I'd find myself standing there talking to a piece of tape. I'd have to imagine who or what I was talking to. Later on, a special-effects person would add something to the film, and then my scene would make sense. It was a different kind of acting for me."

Sometimes, Tom would find himself talking to animals in *Legend*. They didn't always want to cooperate. "In the movie's opening scene, I'm talking to a fox," Tom says. "I'm petting him. But the fox was digging its claws into me. My legs were bleeding as I was doing the scene."

Legend was a physical movie for Tom. "It seemed I was always dropping out of trees and doing gymnastics," Tom says. "The set wasn't level either. That made it harder." The movie set, which cost millions of dollars to build, didn't make it through the movie. During the filming, the set burned to the ground.

The fire was a real setback. It would take weeks to rebuild it. "I remember seeing Ridley walking through the ashes," says Tom. "I walked up to him, but I didn't know what to say. He looked at me and said, 'Well, I'm going to go play some tennis. How about meeting me for dinner later?' Talk about grace under pressure."

Tom waited until the set was rebuilt and finished his work on the movie. By the time it was done, *Legend* had cost $30 million. "I look back on *Legend,* and I'm proud of it," says Tom. "But I don't want to make another movie like that again. I'm glad I did it because I loved watching that kind of movie when I was growing up. It was a good experience for me as an actor, but I know now that I couldn't do another one. There were so many things that were out of my control.

"When I look at *Legend,* I think of the experience I had making it. I think of how I grew as a person and as an actor. I think of what I learned and I learned a lot. It was exciting at the time, but it also made me very hungry to work with a group of actors again. I couldn't wait to start breaking

"I don't want to make another movie like that again."

Tom says the film **Legend** was a challenge both because of the character [a forest man] and because it was a special-effects film."

down scenes again and getting involved with real characters.''

Tom didn't have to wait long. The movie offers were pouring in. Tom kept busy reading scripts. There was one film that really interested him. It was a movie about a group of Navy fighter pilots.

"I don't want to make another movie like that again."

Glossary

This glossary gives an explanation of how certain words were used in this book. A more complete definition of each word can be found in a dictionary.

anxious: looking forward.

ashes: what's left after a fire burns.

battles: fights with.

cancer operation: having a cancer taken out.

challenge: something hard to do.

claws: sharp nails of an animal.

concern: caring about someone.

control: what he had power over.

cooperate: work well with others.

cost: how much money it took.

creature: strange living thing.

decided: made up his mind.

elves: small, make-believe people.

emotionally: having to do with feelings.

exciting: fun.

explain: make something clear.

fairies: make-believe people with magical powers.

fairy tale: made-up story.

fall back on: rely on.

forest man: man who lives in the woods.

goals: things he wants to do in his life.

grace: calmness.

gymnastics: exercises that require a lot of balance and strength.

hospital: place where sick people are cared for.

hungry: wanting something very much.

imagine: picture in his mind.

influence: something that affected him.

innocence: something simple and pure.

level: flat and even.

pilots: people who fly airplanes.

pouring in: coming in all at once.

pressure: a lot to think about.

rebuild: build again.

scariest: made him afraid.

script: what actors say, written down.

setback: something that got in their way.

special-effects: sounds and scenes created by people making the film.

teens: age 13 to 19.

CHAPTER **9**

"Flying in the F–14 seems bigger than life itself."

The movie was *Top Gun*. Like all movies, *Top Gun* started out as an idea. The idea came to Don Simpson and Jerry Bruckheimer, two movie producers. *Flashdance* and *Beverly Hills Cop* had been hit movies for them, and they wanted to make another. When they saw an article in a magazine about the flying school at San Diego's Miramar Naval Air Station, Don and Jerry decided to visit the school.

Some of the best pilots in the world are trained to fly Navy fighter jets at Miramar. Don and Jerry stood and watched as the pilots walked across the runway to their planes. "Those guys look like Tom Cruise," they said to each other. Don and Jerry knew they wanted to make a movie about jet pilots. They also knew they wanted to get Tom to play the leading role.

Later that year, Don and Jerry took a raft trip down the Colorado River. Tony Scott, a British

When the Top Gun *producers visited the Miramar Naval Air Station and watched the pilots training, they said, ''Those guys look like Tom Cruise.''*

director who had made a film called *The Haunting,* also was on the trip. Tony, whose brother Ridley was directing Tom in *Legend,* listened to Don and Jerry talk about the movie they wanted to make. Before long, Tony was chosen as the director of *Top Gun.*

The movie-makers still needed to convince Tom to star in the film. They sent him a script. "I liked it," says Tom, "but it needed a lot of work. I was worried." He met with Don and Jerry and made them an unusual offer. Tom wanted to work on the script before deciding whether or not to be in the movie. "I told them that I'd work on it with them for two months, and even if I didn't decide to make the picture, the script would still be in good shape for someone else. I think I surprised them a little, but after my experience with *Legend,* I wanted to make sure that everything was going to go the way we talked about it."

The producers agreed, and Tom went to work on the script. After a while, he visited Miramar and went for a ride in an F-14 jet. That was all it took. Tom told Don and Jerry he'd take the part. He would become Lieutenant Pete 'Maverick' Mitchell, a Navy jet fighter pilot.

"I hung out with the fighter pilots for nine months," says Tom. "All of them talked to me. They're very emotional about what they do. Those guys go up there and risk their lives every day, and I understood why they do it. Flying in the

F–14 seems bigger than life itself. It is very intense and emotional.

"I love flying the F–14. I'm not big on weapons of war, but I enjoy flying. That's what *Top Gun* is about: the love of flight, the love of competition. It isn't a war movie. I got into the character of those guys and tried to find out what makes them fly.

"The key to Maverick is his love of flight, his wanting to be the best, and his love of competition. None of us wanted to make a war picture. It does take place in a military setting, and because of that, people might say that it's about war. But it isn't. It's a film about Maverick. He isn't a fighter pilot because he wants combat. It's the flying; it's the F–14; it's wanting to be the best.

"I can identify with Maverick, with his desire to be the best. As an actor, I compete with myself all of the time. I challenge myself. I want to be the best at what I do. I want to be the best that I can be."

Tom's best was very good. *Top Gun* was a smash success, a number-one box office draw for weeks. As soon as he was finished working on *Top Gun*, Tom started work on another film. This one was called *The Color Of Money*.

"Flying in the F-14 seems bigger than life itself."

When discussing his character in Top Gun Tom says, "I can identify with Maverick, with his desire to be the best. I want to be the best I can be."

Glossary

This glossary gives an explanation of how certain words were used in this book. A more complete definition of each word can be found in a dictionary.

agreed: felt the same way.

article: a short piece of writing.

chosen: picked.

combat: fighting in war.

compete: to work against others to be the best.

competition: working against others to be the best.

convince: make Tom agree with them.

desire: wanting something.

draw: brought people to the movie theater.

emotional: feel strongly.

good shape: ready.

idea: a thought.

identify: put himself in Maverick's place.

intense: deeply felt.

key: main thing.

magazine: collection of written pieces that comes out every so often.

Navy fighter jets: Navy war planes.

raft: small boat.

risk: do something dangerous.

runway: strip that planes use for taking off and landing.

setting: place.

"Flying in the F–14 seems bigger than life itself."

smash: huge.

surprised: did something not expected.

unusual: different.

war picture: a film about war.

weapons: things used to fight in war.

worried: afraid about what might happen.

CHAPTER **10**

"Tom has got guts and great instinct as an actor."

The Color Of Money was just what Tom had been looking for. "While I was doing *Top Gun*, I was thinking that I'd really like to work with an established, older actor whom I could learn from," he says. "I also wanted to work with an established director. Then Martin Scorsese called me and said he wanted me to read the script for *The Color Of Money*."

Martin Scorsese is a very well-known director. He has made many great films, including *Taxi Driver* and *After Hours*. Paul Newman already had agreed to act in *The Color Of Money*. Paul Newman had starred in *The Hustler*, a 1961 movie about pool hustlers. *The Color Of Money* would be a sequel to *The Hustler*. Paul would play the part of Fast Eddie, the same character he played in *The Hustler*, and he would be given an Oscar for best actor of the year.

"I read the script and saw that there was a role in it for me," says Tom. "I told Marty how much

After **Top Gun,** *Tom wanted to work with an established director. He was pleased when Martin Scorsese offered him a part in* **The Color Of Money.** *"Marty is an actor's director," says Tom.*

I enjoyed the script, and he asked me if I wanted to do it. I said, 'I'd love to!' Then I got busy learning to shoot pool.''

Paul Newman had learned how to shoot pool when he acted in *The Hustler,* but Tom had never played pool before. The movie studio hired Michael Sigel, a champion pool player, to coach both Tom and Paul. Paul was impressed by how quickly Tom learned the game. "It took me a long time to become just OK," says Paul. "It took Tom very little time to get very good."

"Tom has got guts and great instinct as an actor."

Tom played Vincent, a young pool player whom Fast Eddie wants to make into a champion pool hustler. "Fast Eddie is a corrupt hustler," says Tom. "To him, any means justify the end. But Vincent is a pure pool player. Fast Eddie says, 'Man, I'm going to make a lot of money off this kid,' and Eddie tries to turn him into a hustler. Vincent, on the other hand, is riding a crest in life, and nothing can beat him. After a while, Fast Eddie sees what he's been missing."

Paul and Tom became good friends during the filming. "Working with Paul was the greatest," Tom says. "I mean, look at the career that guy has had. He's had high highs and low lows, and he's lasted 30 years. He lives a normal life. He's got a wife and family. He's got several businesses. That was good for me to see."

Paul enjoyed working with Tom, too. "Tom has got guts and great instinct as an actor," says Paul. "He has a real physical sense of his characters. Tom really attacks his scenes."

"It was an honor to work with Paul Newman and Martin Scorsese," says Tom. "Marty is an actor's director. Details, details, details. But I never felt any pressure. We would rehearse, and Marty would adjust his camera shots to the actors. He's very careful and precise about everything he does. The cameras never got in the way of the actors."

The Color Of Money was another hit movie. Once again, Tom had done a great job of acting. Once again, he was ready to move on to something else.

Glossary

This glossary gives an explanation of how certain words were used in this book. A more complete definition of each word can be found in a dictionary.

adjust: change.

attacks: throws himself into.

businesses: ways of making money.

camera shots: pictures taken in making the movie.

career: lifetime job.

corrupt: bad.

crest: high point.

details: picky little things.

established: has been working a long time.

guts: willingness to try new things.

hired: gave a job to.

honor: feeling of pride.

hustlers: people who cheat.

impressed: thought.

instinct: a feel for something.

justify: make it OK.

normal: regular; like other people.

precise: very careful.

pure: interested only in the game.

rehearse: practice.

sequel: movie that follows another.

shoot pool: play pool.

studio: company that made the movie.

"Tom has got guts and great instinct as an actor."

Waving to fans, Tom appeared at the opening of The Color Of Money in New York City to benefit the Actors Studio.

CHAPTER 11

"You have to have the courage to make your own decisions."

Tom is proud of what he has done with his life. "I work very hard," he says. "My craft is the most important thing in my life. I'm still trying to grow as an actor and as a person."

With regard to Tom's personal life, it doesn't look like he is thinking about getting married. "I've had a few serious girl friends, and I go out on dates, but I've never thought that I wanted to be married," he says. "I do like women. Women are terrific. I should know, after all, I grew up in a house full of them. I saw how men treated them, and I talked to them and found out how they felt about it. My mother and sisters are interesting, unique people. When I was growing up, they were my best friends. I'm very careful with the women I date. I treat them the way I would want my sisters to be treated."

As an actor, Tom says, "I need to have a lot of things happening in my life. I would like to direct,

Shown here with friend Mimi Rogers, Tom says, "Women are terrific. I should know, after all, I grew up in a house full of them."

"Have the courage to make your own decisions."

but I'm not ready for that just yet. I enjoy working with writers and their scripts; it's very exciting to me. Someday, I would like to produce, direct, and act onstage, but I don't feel a heavy pressure to do those things right now. When I do them, I want to do them well."

For now, Tom is too busy being an actor to find much time for anything else. He has his own production company, which takes even more time out of his life. "Sometimes, I'm working so much that I'm alone 95 percent of the time," Tom says. "It's tough having a relationship with anyone because when I'm doing a film, that's all I think about."

Does Tom have any advice for other actors who want to become better at what they do? "Yes," he says. "Take big risks. You have to. I'm always looking for characters that will help me grow. I want my characters to be fresh and real, so it's a constant search.

"What makes an actor's performance interesting are the choices he or she makes. Once I've done something, I don't want to do it again. That just bores me and the audience. I like feeling nervous and excited about my roles. When I find good material, it wakes me up. It's exciting, but I always ask myself why I would want to make the film. What does it offer me? What do I have to offer it? Because of that attitude, each thing I've done has helped me grow.

"I've got a strong point of view, and I like to get it across in the films I do. I think that's important, too."

As he's said before, Tom knows that he's been lucky. "I told Paul Newman that," Tom says. "Do you know what he said to me? 'There's an art to being lucky.' "

"But it takes more than luck to succeed as an actor. Look at Paul Newman. He's made about 60 movies. *The Color Of Money* was my eighth. If I want to do what he's done, it will take more than luck. I only hope that when I'm his age, I'll be playing the kind of great parts that he still is.

"With every film I make, I can feel myself becoming more and more relaxed. I'm a good listener, and I think that helps. Not that I take all the advice I get, but I listen and learn. You have to do that, and you have to have the courage to make your own decisions. Then . . . you have to go for it.

"Someone, I think it was Spencer Tracy, once said, 'Acting is great. Just don't ever let anyone catch you doing it.' That's very true. The important thing is to be relaxed in your work. It's the same in life. Don't make everything too intense. Then you can let everything go and not have to 'act' at all. That's the way I want to be."

"Have the courage to make your own decisions."

Tom's advice for actors who want to improve their skills, "Take big risks. I'm always looking for characters that will help me grow. I want my characters to be fresh and real."

Glossary

This glossary gives an explanation of how certain words were used in this book. A more complete definition of each word can be found in a dictionary.

advice: what others tell him.
art: talent.
attitude: what he thinks about something.
bores: makes him tired.
choices: what someone decides to do.
constant: all of the time.
courage: ability to face difficult things.
craft: job that requires great skill.
decisions: what someone chooses to do.
grow: learn.
heavy: hard to bear.
intense: serious.
married: joined together; husband and wife.
material: scripts.
nervous: a little afraid.
performance: acting.
point of view: way of looking at things.
relationship: friendship with another person.
relaxed: not afraid.
risks: a choice that can turn out good or bad.
search: looking everywhere.
serious: steady; long-term.

"Have the courage to make your own decisions."

succeed: make it.
terrific: wonderful.
unique: one of a kind.
wakes: gives him energy.